RECORDING

Scott Witmer

VISIT US AT
WWW.ABDOPUBLISHING.COM

Published by ABDO Publishing Company, 8000 West 78th Street, Suite 310, Edina, MN 55439. Copyright ©2010 by Abdo Consulting Group, Inc. International copyrights reserved in all countries. No part of this book may be reproduced in any form without written permission from the publisher. ABDO & Daughters™ is a trademark and logo of ABDO Publishing Company.

Printed in the United States.

 PRINTED ON RECYCLED PAPER

Editor: John Hamilton
Graphic Design: Sue Hamilton
Cover Design: John Hamilton
Cover Photo: iStockphoto
Interior Photos and Illustrations: AP-pgs 7 & 24; Apple-GarageBand-pg 20; Boss-Digital Recording Studio-pg 18; Cheap Trick-pg 22; Corbis-pg 15; Digidesign-Pro Tools-pg 21; Getty Images-pgs 10, 11, 12, 13, 14, 17, 19, 23, & 27; iStockphoto-pgs 4, 5, 25, 26 & 29; Jupiterimages-pgs 1, 3, 6, 9, 16, & 31; Lane-Microphone-pg 28; Library of Congress-pgs 6 & 8, Talking Heads-pg 23; and Wikimedia-Morio-Nippon Budokan-pg 22.

Library of Congress Cataloging-in-Publication Data

Witmer, Scott.
  Recording / Scott Witmer.
     p. cm. -- (Rock band)
  Includes index.
  ISBN 978-1-60453-694-2
  1. Rock music--Vocational guidance--Juvenile literature. 2. Sound recordings--Production and direction--Juvenile literature. I. Title.
  ML3795.W528 2009
  781.66'149--dc22
                              2009006611

CONTENTS

SOUND REPRODUCTION

For most of human history, the only way to hear music was to attend a live performance or concert. Only in the past 130 years or so have we been able to record live performances and play them back later.

The process of capturing live music and transferring it to some other medium is called "recording." Normally, this takes place in a specialized building or room called a recording studio. The goal is to reproduce, as accurately as possible, the sound of a live performance. Through the years, technology has brought us closer and closer to hearing exactly what the music sounded like when it was originally played live.

> A singer working in a recording studio.

Specialized audio equipment is used for recording live bands.

In 1877, American inventor Thomas Edison developed the phonograph. It used a thin, speaker-like device called a diaphragm, which had a small needle attached to it. The needle was held against a piece of tin foil wrapped around a rotating cylinder. When somebody sang or played an instrument into a mouthpiece, the sound waves caused the diaphragm to vibrate, which then made the needle etch a pattern of grooves into the tin foil.

A young Thomas Edison shows off his phonograph in April 1878.

To play the recorded sound back, the process worked in reverse: the grooves in the cylinder caused the diaphragm to vibrate, which re-created the original sound through a megaphone attached to the machine. It was primitive, but it worked.

Building on Edison's success, German immigrant Emile Berliner in the late 1880s found a way to record sound onto small spinning disks instead of rotating cylinders. Berliner called his invention the gramophone. The disks, or records, were easier to mass-produce, and more convenient when storing large collections of music. By the early 1900s, almost all music was produced on spinning disks. It was a technology that would be refined and improved for decades, remaining popular until the 1980s, when it was finally made obsolete by the invention of digital music stored on compact disks (CDs).

The gramophone used spinning disks.

In 2009, the rock group Coldplay received a Best Rock Album Grammy Award for *Viva la Vida*. Grammy Awards are presented each year by the National Academy of Recording Arts and Sciences.

The Grammys

The Grammy Awards are widely considered to be the most prestigious musical award in the United States. The awards are presented each year by the National Academy of Recording Arts and Sciences. The Grammy gets it names from the gramophone.

RECORDING MUSIC

In the early days of recorded music, band members played their instruments into a large megaphone. The sound caused a needle to vibrate, which cut grooves into a spinning master disk. The master disk was later used to mass-produce duplicate records for sale. If mistakes were made during recording, the musicians would have to start over, and a new disk would have to be cut. It is said that you could tell how well rehearsed a band was by the size of the pile of disk shavings that were left over after the recording process was finally complete.

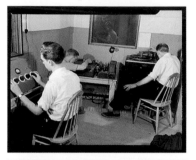

In 1942, equipment operators cut a musical recording with a recording machine. The master disk was then used to duplicate the recording onto other records.

In the early 20th century, electric microphones were invented, and recorded music started to become more sophisticated.

> Violinist Renee Chemet stands by a carbon microphone. Inventors Emile Berliner and Thomas Edison filed for patents on carbon microphones within weeks of each other in April 1878. Many lawsuits ensued, but were settled out of court. Eventually, the carbon microphone became the industry standard, and was used in the early years of radio.

In addition to using microphones, speakers, and amplifiers, the process of cutting "directly to disk" gave way to recording on magnetic tape. This recording medium used long, narrow strips of flexible plastic with a magnetic coating, usually iron oxide. The tape was moved past a "writing head," which recorded a magnetic signal onto the coating. The signal mimicked the fluctuations and volume of the original sound waves captured by the microphone. This type of process is called "analog" tape recording, and was heavily used in recording music up until the mid-1980s.

> Recording on magnetic tape, or analog tape recording, was used in the music industry up until the mid-1980s.

A big breakthrough in analog tape recording was the use of "multi-track" recording. A track refers to a particular section of the tape. Each musician in a band can record on a separate track. The results are then mixed, or volume adjusted, to create a better-quality recording.

The first multi-track recorders required that all the band members play together, with separate microphones placed in the studio. Eventually, the process developed so that musicians could play their parts separately at different times. For example, a drummer and bass guitarist could "lay down" their tracks. Later, the band's guitarist could come into the studio. Listening to a recording of the drums and bass on headphones, he or she could lay down the guitar part on a separate track. Then, an audio engineer in the studio would mix all the parts together to create a complete song.

Multi-track recording is very handy for vocalists. If a band's singer forgets a lyric or makes some other kind of mistake, the entire band does not have to replay the song. The vocalist can go back and re-record the part of the song where the mistake was made, saving everyone else a lot of time.

As multi-track recorders became popular, individual musicians could record their parts separately.

A digital recording studio.

Multi-track recording has evolved from two tracks in the early days, to virtually unlimited tracks in modern studios. The process of putting recordings on analog tape has given way to digital recording. Instead of a continuous, analog signal, digital recording only needs two magnetic states—on or off, positive or negative. By combining millions of such signals, digital hardware can record and play back music with high accuracy. Another big advantage of digital is that duplication of the master recording is flawless, with copies sounding as good as the original.

Today, most digital recording is done on hard drives with the aid of computers. Digital recording is much easier than tape to edit, store, and manipulate. Also, the audio engineer or producer who controls the sound mixing can much more easily jump to sections of a song in the digital medium than was possible with analog tape, which greatly speeds up the creative process.

MODERN STUDIOS

In the early days of recording, studios were large spaces with distinctive acoustic properties. Very large rooms had a kind of echo-like quality that resembled a concert hall. Performing in old churches, for example, produced desirable sounds that could be captured on a recording.

As technology advanced, recording studios added smaller rooms that captured a true unaffected sound, which could later be manipulated after recording. Echo could be added later, as well as other effects and sound adjustments.

> As technology advanced, recording studios went from large open spaces with an echo-like quality, to small rooms that captured true unaffected sound.

> McFly rock band members Tom Fletcher (left) and Dan Jones (right) recording in a studio in London, England.

A typical studio setup today has a "live" room, where musicians play into microphones, and a separate control room, or "mixing booth," that contains all of the electronics necessary for recording. The two rooms are usually separated by glass, and feature an intercom that the producer or sound engineer can use to speak with the band between recording takes. Advanced studios feature separate rooms, called "isolation booths," that allow different instruments or vocalists to be separated from the other members of the band during recording. This helps record the purest sound possible. For example, keeping a drummer in an isolation booth prevents the drum sound from "bleeding through" into a guitarist's track.

A sound engineer at work.

The person in charge of operating the complicated equipment in the studio is commonly called an engineer. More specifically, these skilled people are called sound engineers, audio engineers, or recording engineers. The engineer controls the placement of microphones in the live room, and monitors and adjusts the sound being recorded in the control room. For smaller studios, the engineer will also mix the final recordings.

Mixing is the process in which the final tracks are adjusted and manipulated to obtain the best possible sound. For example, the drum sound may need to be louder in certain parts of the song than others. Mixing is also the part of the process where any additional effects, such as echo or reverb, are added to the recording material.

The final mix must then be "mastered," or prepared, for the final media in which it is to be distributed and sold. For example, there are certain adjustments needed to make sure the final mix will sound good when transferred to a CD.

After recording music, the final step is to adjust and mix the tracks for the best possible sound. The final mix will be the master from which copies are made, such as CDs.

Large record companies and artists with big record contracts usually have several people who oversee this entire process. The sound engineer may be a different person than the mixing engineer. There might also be a separate person who oversees the mastering of the recording.

Most big-name acts will also have a record producer. A producer oversees all aspects of recording, from the arrangement of the songs to the final mastering of the final mix. However, in small studios that are available to new bands, or bands on a budget, the recording engineer will handle all of these tasks. Most recording engineers are very capable in all areas of music production.

Studio time can be very expensive for recording artists at the top of the industry. Hiring producers and engineers, plus renting the studio and necessary equipment, can quickly add up to big dollars. However, for bands on a budget, there are many mid-level studios that can be more affordable. It is possible to obtain quality studio time for $150 to $250 per hour. Even so, it is obviously very helpful to a band's budget if they are well rehearsed before entering the recording studio.

 Studio time can be very expensive. It's important that band members be well rehearsed and ready to perform as soon as they enter the recording studio.

A great deal of training is needed to become a professional sound or mixing engineer.

HOME RECORDING

New advances in technology have created very inexpensive, yet powerful, home recording devices. These new home studios have allowed bands on a budget to skip the cost of a traditional recording studio and instead record music at home. Recording equipment that even 20 years ago could have cost hundreds of thousands of dollars can now be had for under $1,000.

For bands interested in recording at home, there are many choices. The most popular options are purchasing a stand-alone recording device, or purchasing software for a home computer.

Stand-alone multi-track recorders are specialized electronic devices made just for recording music. About the size of a briefcase, they have several inputs for plugging in guitars, microphones, or other electric instruments. A stand-alone recorder is very useful because its sole purpose is the recording and mixing of audio. They are pre-loaded with the software and connections you need for this purpose. They are also integrated, which means all of the amps and connections are already built in, so you don't have to worry about connections between components—everything is already set up for you. Stand-alone units also have real knobs and levers on them. Many people find it easier to perform their final mix with physical knobs, instead of using a computer interface.

> A BOSS stand-alone multi-track recorder with a built-in CD burner is advertised as "the musician's portable power studio." It allows the user to write, record, edit, mix, master, and burn a complete finished CD.

Moby has a home recording studio, as do many professional musicians.

Today, most stand-alone multi-track recorders are digital recorders, meaning that they record to digital media, such as a hard disk or digital tape. Earlier recorders used analog tape, sometimes called "reel-to-reel." Digital media is much easier to access, edit, and store. It is also possible to store much more data on a digital hard drive than a reel-to-reel tape, so more tracks are possible, and recording quality is greatly improved. Most current multi-track recorders feature at least 8 tracks of recording, with some models going up to 32 tracks or more. Consumer-grade multi-track recorders usually cost under $1,000. Some entry-level four-track models can be found for under $200.

Using computer software to record a band's music has become increasingly popular. With such programs as Digidesign's Pro Tools, Cakewalk Sonar, and Apple's Logic Studio, musicians are using the power of their home computers to create great demos and albums. Home recording software has become so popular that Apple pre-loads GarageBand, a very capable home recording application, on every computer the company sells.

GARAGE BAND

> Apple computers come pre-loaded with the home recording software, GarageBand.

PRO TOOLS

> Digidesign's Pro Tools is computer software designed to allow musicians to achieve recordings with professional results, all on a personal computer.

There are many advantages of using computer software to record your band's music. Recording software will often have unlimited track recording capability. The tracks that can be recorded at one time are usually only limited by the processing power of the computer itself. Recording software has unlimited expandability and flexibility. Any number of devices can be plugged into a computer, and any number of additional software sounds and effects can be downloaded or added.

Recording software is usually much more robust and feature-filled than a stand-alone multi-track recorder. That means your ability to edit, cut, splice, and polish music is greater on a computer than it would be on a stand-alone unit. Good-quality home recording software usually costs under $500 when purchased in a retail store.

LIVE RECORDING

Although studio albums are the most common type of recording to be released, many musicians feel that live performances are the best way to experience their music. Live performances can be much more exciting, and "real," than a studio recording. This is why people spend hundreds of dollars a seat to see top-name artists on stage. However, recording a live performance holds many risks. There can be equipment failure, band member missteps, and any number of mistakes or mishaps that can occur during a live performance. If a guitar player blows a solo in a live recording, he can't go back and re-record it like he can in the studio. These risks may also heighten the excitement of a live recording.

Many classic albums are recordings of live performances, including Cheap Trick's *Live at Budokan*, the Talking Heads' *Stop Making Sense*, and The Who's *Live at Leeds*. All of these albums are classic rock performances. They capture the spirit of the band, providing a snapshot of exactly what the group sounded like at that particular time. This is what most bands strive for when recording a live album.

CHEAP TRICK

> Cheap Trick recorded *Live at Budokan* at the Nippon Budokan arena in Tokyo, Japan, in 1978. Many rock groups played and recorded at this famous stadium.

TALKING HEADS

> In December 1983, the Talking Heads recorded three of their live performances in Hollywood, California. They created a concert movie of the footage, and then released the soundtrack. The *Stop Making Sense* album came out in 1984.

Professional sound technicians and sound engineers coordinate all the necessary equipment to make sure the musicians are properly heard and recorded.

Big-name bands that attempt to record live performances have a dedicated team of sound technicians and sound engineers. This team plugs directly into the venue's soundboard and receives all tracks from the music being played on stage. They will then mix this sound with professional-grade equipment, preserving every aspect of the performance and keeping the sound quality at the highest possible level.

When newer bands want to record live performances, their options are somewhat limited. When recording live, it is much easier if there is a professional public address or PA system in the venue. Normally, sound technicians running the soundboard on the PA will let the band "plug in," or record the sound from the PA. This can be done with any type of recording device, from a cassette recorder to a digital tape recorder, or even a laptop computer. This sound is usually pretty good, as it is the same sound that the audience hears from the PA system.

The downside to this method is that you will not hear much of the crowd noise, and in small venues, the drums will be a bit muted. The sound technician will not normally have to add loud drums into the PA mix in small venues, since they are usually loud enough on their own to fill the room. So, if they aren't in the mix, they won't be on your tape. A very inexpensive solution to this problem is to bring a stand-alone multi-track recorder to the gig. As long as the venue permits it, you can plug into the PA system with two tracks (to maintain a stereo mix), and run one or two microphones above the audience. Using this method, you can get a track that records the audience response and applause, and your crowd microphones will also pick up the drum sounds and enhance them a bit. This isn't a perfect solution, but it will work in a pinch, and on a budget.

A band who wants to make a live recording may be able to plug into a stage's PA system. The sound will then be recorded from the PA.

RECORDING EQUIPMENT

The studio can be a very intimidating place. Even a home studio can be confusing. For a first-time recording band, there are many pieces of equipment that are used that the band may have never encountered before. Rest assured, there will be a sound engineer there to help you, but here is a basic rundown of some common equipment that might be found in a typical studio's control room.

The first thing that almost anyone notices when entering a recording studio's control room is the enormous mixing console. This sophisticated piece of equipment is typically very large, and consists of several vertical sliding fader knobs, and rotating pan knobs. The pan knobs usually control the stereo mix or loudness of a certain track, and the fader knobs control the master volume or recording level of the track. The mixing console is where all of the microphones and inputs from the live room are routed. The console then controls all of the sound that comes out of the recording session. This sound is mixed, adjusted, manipulated, and sent to a multi-track recorder.

Audio Mixing Console

The multi-track recorder records sound that is sent from the mixing console onto either analog tape, or, more common today, digital media. In larger studios, the recorder is usually computer based. The tracks stored on the multi-track recorder can later be played back and edited, then re-mixed before being sent for mastering.

The control room also features several sets of high-quality speakers, which allows the engineer to hear the best possible reproduction of the recorded sound. These speakers are also called monitors, reference speakers, monitor speakers, or studio monitors. These monitors are designed to deliver the most accurate sound

Large, high-quality speakers are mounted on this control room's wall.

possible without distortion. Highly specialized, the studio monitors produce a "flat" sound, which does not have extra bass or treble (low or high) sound frequencies emphasized.

In addition to monitors, the control room might also have several other sets of speakers available that simulate what the recording might sound like when played through other types of speakers. For example, it could simulate what a song might sound like when played back from a stereo in your living room, or from a car stereo.

TIPS AND TRICKS

Remember, recording should be a fun process. When it becomes tedious or frustrating, the final music produced usually suffers. There is no quicker way to stifle your creativity than by feeling that the recording process is a "job."

The most important thing that bands can do to make sure that recording goes well is to be very well rehearsed with the material they intend to record. A band should have a clear plan about which songs they want to put on their record or demo, and then practice them over and over. This will result in far fewer takes in the studio. Less takes mean less overdubs, or "do-overs," and less time spent in the studio. Less time in the studio translates to lower cost.

Bands should also have a clear idea of what to expect from a final mix. Again, the less time that bands spend paying an engineer to mix an album, the lower the studio cost will be.

It is a good idea to use the highest-quality microphone that the band can afford.

If a band is recording at home, then the best advice is to use the highest-quality microphone that the band can afford to buy or rent. High-quality microphones have a higher "frequency response," the range of sound they can record. The nicer the microphone, the better your recordings will usually sound.

Bands should also familiarize themselves as much as possible with their dedicated hardware or computer software before they attempt to record music. This will result in less time spent recording, and less wasted time when it comes to mixing.

Recording should be a fun process. Being well-rehearsed and ready to play creates great music.

GLOSSARY

ACOUSTIC

When an instrument is played without electronic amplification to make the sound louder. The sound made by the vibrating strings of an acoustic guitar are made louder by resonating inside the hollow body of the instrument.

DISTORTION

When the amplified signal from an electric guitar is "overdriven," which "clips" the signal and results in a kind of gritty, screaming buzz that is popular with hard rock musicians.

GIG

A job as a musician.

GRAMMY AWARD

Yearly awards given out by the National Academy of Recording Arts and Sciences to outstanding artists in various musical categories. The award is named after the gramophone, an early record player.

MASTER

An original recording from which copies can be made.

MULTI-TRACK RECORDER

A device that allows for the recording of instruments or voices separately, as individual "tracks." The individual tracks are then fed through a mixing console, which combines the tracks to create a clean, clear sound.

RECORDING STUDIO

A place for recording sounds, such as music or the spoken word. Usually, a recording studio will be divided into two or more rooms. The "studio" is the place where a person or persons go to speak, play, or sing. The "control room" holds all the technical recording equipment. A recording studio may also have one or more "isolation booths," which are rooms where artists playing louder instruments, such as drums, are recorded separately. By keeping loud instruments separate, their sound doesn't mingle with that of the other artists. This makes for a cleaner recording.

REVERB

Reverberation, often called reverb, is when a sound continues to be heard even after the source has stopped producing noise. When a loud, continuous sound is created in an enclosed space (like a music hall), echoes can build up. When the instrument making the music stops, the series of echoes continue to bounce around the space, slowly decaying until they can no longer be heard. Reverb in rock music today is often used as a desirable effect, and can easily be produced with modern amplifiers.

SOUNDBOARD

Sound mixing equipment, also known as a mixing console. It is used to mix all the different voices and instruments into a unified, clear sound.

STUDIO MONITORS

High-quality speakers used in a recording studio's control room. They allow a sound engineer to hear the best possible reproduction of the recorded sound. These speakers are also called monitors, reference speakers, or monitor speakers.

INDEX